MH-53J PAVE LOWS

BY CARLOS ALVAREZ

BELLWETHER MEDIA · MINNEAPOLIS, MN

Are you ready to take it to the extreme?
Torque books thrust you into the action-packed
world of sports, vehicles, and adventure. These books
may include dirt, smoke, fire, and dangerous stunts.
WARNING: read at your own risk.

Library of Congress Cataloging-in-Publication Data

Alvarez, Carlos, 1968-
  MH-53J Pave Lows / by Carlos Alvarez.
      p. cm. – (Torque: military machines)
  Summary: "Amazing photography accompanies engaging information about MH-53J Pave Lows.
The combination of high-interest subject matter and light text is intended for students in grades 3
through 7"–Provided by publisher.
  Includes bibliographical references and index.
  ISBN 978-1-60014-281-9 (hardcover : alk. paper)
  1. Sikorsky H-53 (Military transport helicopter)–Juvenile literature. 2. United States. Air Force–
Search and rescue operations–Juvenile literature. I. Title.
  UG1232.T72A46 2010
  623.74'65–dc22   2009008489

This edition first published in 2010 by Bellwether Media, Inc..

The photographs in this book are reproduced through the courtesy of: United States Department of
Defense, front cover, pp. 4-5, 6, 7, 8-9, 10-11, 12, 13, 16, 17, 18, 19, 20, 20-21; Ted Carlson / Fotodynamics, 14-15.

Printed in the United States of America.

CONTENTS

THE MH-53J IN ACTION

The low hum of helicopter **rotors** fills the air. A United States Air Force MH-53J Pave Low flies into view. It is on a **mission** to pick up special operations troops. They are deep behind enemy lines.

The enemy spots the Pave Low. They fire at the helicopter. Their bullets can't get through its thick **armor**. A machine gun from one side of the Pave Low returns fire. It sends the enemy running. The MH-53J quickly touches down. Six U.S. troops run out from hiding. They climb into the helicopter. The Pave Low rises quickly and speeds back to base.

LONG-RANGE INFILTRATOR

The MH-53J Pave Low was built to carry troops or equipment deep into enemy territory. It carried U.S. troops into and out of combat. The Pave Low could fly low enough to hide from enemy **radar**. Its huge fuel tanks gave it a range of more than 690 miles (1,110 kilometers).

★ FAST FACT ★

The MH-53J can carry two external fuel tanks. Each tank holds 450 gallons (1,700 liters) of fuel.

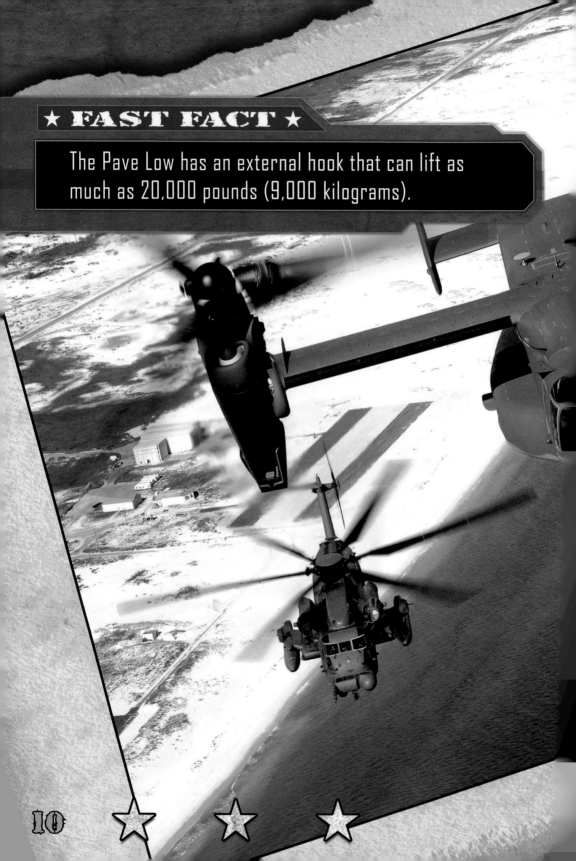

The Pave Low has an external hook that can lift as much as 20,000 pounds (9,000 kilograms).

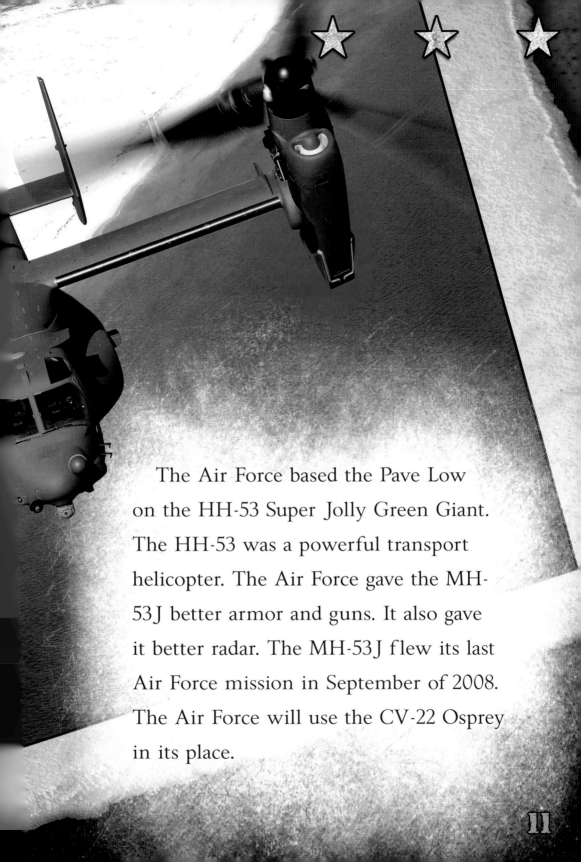

The Air Force based the Pave Low on the HH-53 Super Jolly Green Giant. The HH-53 was a powerful transport helicopter. The Air Force gave the MH-53J better armor and guns. It also gave it better radar. The MH-53J flew its last Air Force mission in September of 2008. The Air Force will use the CV-22 Osprey in its place.

WEAPONS AND FEATURES

The Pave Low is equipped for combat. It has a gun mount on each side. It also has one in the rear. Each mount can hold a 7.62mm **minigun** or a .50 caliber machine gun. A minigun can fire thousands of bullets per minute.

The Pave Low is built to keep its crew and passengers safe. Its metal armor protects it from enemy fire. Extra-strong **titanium** armor protects the cockpit and fuel tanks. The Pave Low also has the ability to launch **countermeasures**. These confuse heat-seeking **missiles**.

IRONHORSE
21

★ FAST FACT ★

The United States Navy uses a variant of the Pave Low called the CH-53E Super Stallion.

Communication on the battlefield is important. The Pave Low has equipment to jam enemy radio and radar signals. Secure radio communication gear prevents enemies from detecting the MH-53J's radio signals. This helps Pave Lows complete their missions.

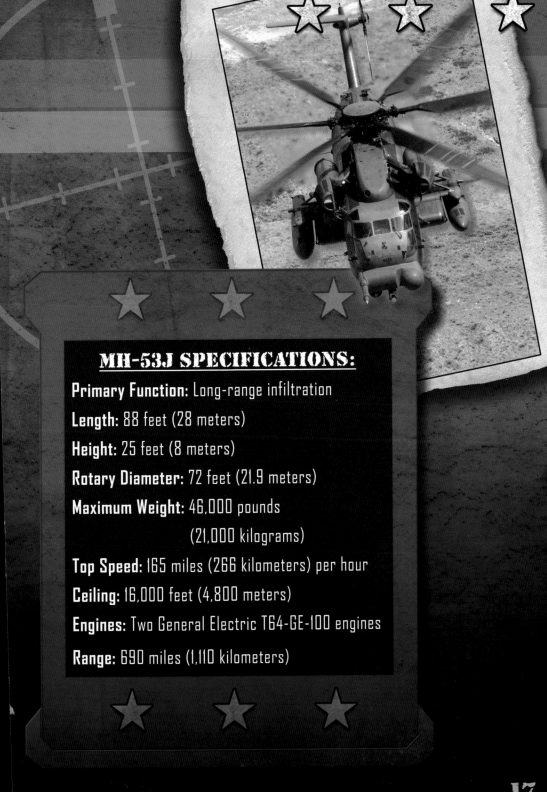

MH-53J SPECIFICATIONS:

Primary Function: Long-range infiltration

Length: 88 feet (28 meters)

Height: 25 feet (8 meters)

Rotary Diameter: 72 feet (21.9 meters)

Maximum Weight: 46,000 pounds
(21,000 kilograms)

Top Speed: 165 miles (266 kilometers) per hour

Ceiling: 16,000 feet (4,800 meters)

Engines: Two General Electric T64-GE-100 engines

Range: 690 miles (1,110 kilometers)

MH-53J MISSIONS

The MH-53J has three primary missions. It inserts troops into enemy territory. It also brings supplies to troops behind enemy lines. Sometimes it picks up or rescues troops behind enemy lines. All three missions are extremely dangerous.

19

A Pave Low has six crew members. It can carry up to 38 troops. Two pilots share the flying duties. Two **flight engineers** control the electronic systems. Two gunners operate the weapons. The crew is often deep behind enemy lines. They need to work as a team to stay safe. They cannot relax until they are safely back to base.

GLOSSARY

armor—protective metal covering

countermeasure—a defensive device, such as a flare, designed to confuse the guidance system of an enemy weapon

flight engineer—a crew member in charge of operating an MH-53J's electronic systems

minigun—a multi-barreled machine gun with a very high rate of fire

missile—an explosive launched at targets on the ground or in the air

mission—a military task

radar—a sensor system that uses radio waves to locate objects

rotor—the set of rotating blades above a helicopter that gives it lift

titanium—a strong, lightweight metal sometimes used in armor plating

TO LEARN MORE

AT THE LIBRARY

David, Jack. *HH-60 Pave Hawk Helicopters*.
Minneapolis, Minn.: Bellwether, 2009.

Sweetman, Bill. *Combat Rescue Helicopters: The MH-53 Pave Lows*. Mankato, Minn.: Capstone, 2008.

Zobel, Derek. *United States Air Force*. Minneapolis, Minn.: Bellwether, 2008.

ON THE WEB

Learning more about military machines is as easy as 1, 2, 3.

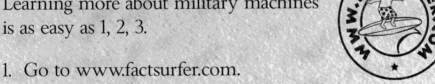

1. Go to www.factsurfer.com.

2. Enter "military machines" into search box.

3. Click the "Surf" button and you will see a list of related Web sites.

With factsurfer.com, finding more information is just a click away.

INDEX